D1299215

Waterfalls

Rourke
Educational Media

rourkeeducationalmedia.com

Precious McKenzie

Before & After Reading Activities

Teaching Focus:
Fluency: Encourage extensive reading and use specific methods, such as timed readings, and partner reading to stimulate growth in fluency.

Before Reading:

Building Academic Vocabulary and Background Knowledge
Before reading a book, it is important to set the stage for your child or student by using pre-reading strategies. This will help them develop their vocabulary, increase their reading comprehension, and make connections across the curriculum.

1. *Read the title and look at the cover. Let's make predictions about what this book will be about.*
2. *Take a picture walk by talking about the pictures/photographs in the book. Implant the vocabulary as you take the picture walk. Be sure to talk about the text features such as headings, Table of Contents, glossary, bolded words, captions, charts/ diagrams, or Index.*
3. Have students read the first page of text with you then have students read the remaining text.
4. *Strategy Talk – use to assist students while reading.*
   - *Get your mouth ready*
   - *Look at the picture*
   - *Think…does it make sense*
   - *Think…does it look right*
   - *Think…does it sound right*
   - *Chunk it – by looking for a part you know*
5. *Read it again.*

Content Area Vocabulary
Use glossary words in a sentence.

elevation
erodes
ledge
soil

After Reading:

Comprehension and Extension Activity
After reading the book, work on the following questions with your child or students in order to check their level of reading comprehension and content mastery.

1. *What does it mean when land erodes? (Summarize)*
2. *What can cause waterfalls? (Asking Questions)*
3. *Have you ever visited a waterfall? (Text to Self Connection)*
4. *Why are there so many kinds of waterfalls? (Asking Questions)*

Extension Activity
Using modeling clay, build a model of a river, a waterfall, and a plunge pool. You can include rapids, a whirlpool, a ledge, and rocks. Label the parts of the waterfall.

Table of Contents

Falling Water

Sometimes water spills over a cliff or **ledge**. This is called a waterfall.

ledge

On the Move

Any time **soil** moves or **erodes**, a waterfall may form. Volcanoes, earthquakes, and glaciers can make waterfalls.

Changes in **elevation**, erosion, and water flow will make either a large or small waterfall.

River water runs swiftly toward a cliff. This creates rapids. The rushing water moves soil, rocks, logs, and fish.

rapids

Water falling from a ledge lands in a plunge pool. Whirlpools are dangerous circular water currents. They swirl in the plunge pool.

whirlpool

cave

Caves are often found behind waterfalls. The cave is carved by the power of the water.

Let's Classify!

Scientists classify waterfalls. They study how much water falls. They study how high and wide a waterfall is.

They study how much water comes down. Then they decide what type of waterfall it is. There are ten types of waterfalls in the world.

Types of Waterfalls

Block

Cascade

Chute

Cataract

Fan

Frozen

Horsetail

Plunge

Punch Bowl

Multi-step

19

People like to visit waterfalls. But, be careful. Waterfalls are powerful! Some are not safe to hike or swim near.

Waterfall Facts

The tallest waterfall in the world is Angel Falls in Venezuela. Its water falls 3,212 feet (979 meters).

Many waterfalls are used to make electricity.

A waterfall can freeze in cold weather. Then the water stops flowing!

Over time, a waterfall will reshape the land around it.

Picture Glossary

 **elevation** (el-uh-VAY-shuhn): Elevation is measurement of the height of land or how tall a hill or mountain is.

 **erodes** (i-RODEZ): When rock or land is worn away by the elements such as water and wind.

 **ledge** (LEJ): A ledge is a shelf that sticks out from the side of a mountain.

 **soil** (SOYL): The top layer of earth in which plants grow.

Index

Meet The Author!
www.meetREMauthors.com

Websites to Visit

www.scienceforkidsclub.com/waterfalls.html
http://kids.britannica.com/elementary/article-400200/waterfall
www.nationalgeographic.org/encyclopedia/waterfall

About the Author

Precious McKenzie lives in Montana. She loves being outdoors, visiting parks, and sharing Mother Nature with her three children and three dogs.

www.rourkeeducationalmedia.com

PHOTO CREDITS: Cover and title page ©fotojog; p.5 ©Puripat Lertpunyaroj; p.7 ©Ammit Jack; p.8 ©JTobiasonPhoto; p.9 ©DNY59; p.11 ©surangaw; p.13 ©Paolo Costa; p.14-15 ©Rauluminate; p.15 ©Ditty_about_summer; p.17 ©pixfly; p.19 ©Scoast, ©rusm, ©verve231, ©Ralf Hettler, ©Wiki, ©nikpal, ©михаил мандрыгин, ©StockstudioX, ©Justin Horrocks, ©kitchakron; p.20 ©nomadFra; p.23 ©Pash237, ©Csondy, ©pitr134, ©Giselleflissak

Edited by: Keli Sipperley
Cover design by: Nicola Stratford   www.nicolastratford.com
Interior design by: Rhea Magaro-Wallace

Library of Congress PCN Data

Waterfalls / Precious McKenzie
(Mother Nature)
ISBN (hard cover)(alk. paper) 978-1-68342-321-8
ISBN (soft cover) 978-1-68342-417-8
ISBN (e-Book) 978-1-68342-487-1
Library of Congress Control Number: 2017931169

Printed in the United States of America, North Mankato, Minnesota